MEGAN FOX BIOGRAPHY

The Rise of Confident and Controversial Celebrity

Stephanie Pollard

Copyright © 2024 by Stephanie Pollard.

Table of Contents

Introduction

Chapter 1
    Birth and Family Background
    Childhood Experiences and Upbringing
    Early Education and Interests

Chapter 2
  Pursuing Acting
    Introduction to Acting and Early Roles
    Transition to Hollywood
    Challenges and Setbacks

Chapter 3
  Breakthrough with "Transformers"
    Casting as Mikaela Banes
    Impact of "Transformers" on Fox's Caree
    Controversies and Media Attention

Chapter 4
  Filmography
    Analysis of Significant Roles and Performances
  Evolution of Fox's Acting Style

Chapter 5
  Television Career

    Analysis of Significant Roles and Performances

Chapter 6
   Public Image and Persona
      Perception as a Sex Symbol
      Media Scrutiny and Challenges
      Personal Branding and Public Statements
Chapter 7

   Personal Life
      Relationships and Family
      Struggles with Mental Health and Self-esteem
      Philanthropy and Advocacy

Chapter 8
   Beyond Acting
      Other Ventures and Interests
      Impact Beyond the Entertainment Industry
Chapter 9

   Legacy and Influence
      Reflections on Her Career and Contributions

Conclusion

Introduction

Few people have captivated the public's attention as much as Megan Fox in the vibrant city of Hollywood, where dreams are brought to life and stars are created under the intense spotlight. With an allure as potent as it is enigmatic, Fox has transcended the confines of traditional celebrity to become an icon of our times—a symbol of beauty, talent, and unyielding determination in the face of adversity.

However, there is a tale of tenacity, ardor, and unwavering honesty hidden behind the captivating exterior. This book takes us on a journey through Megan Fox's life and career, revealing the person behind the roles, the controversies, and the headlines.

From her humble beginnings in Oak Ridge, Tennessee, to the dazzling heights of Hollywood stardom, Fox's trajectory has been nothing short of extraordinary. We examine the hardships and struggles that molded her into the strong woman she is today as we delve into her early years. Raised in a strict household and navigating the tumultuous waters of adolescence, Fox's journey to success was fraught with challenges—but through it all, she remained steadfast in her pursuit of her dreams.

Through this book, we will discover the key events that shaped Fox's career, from her breakthrough performance in

"Transformers" to her wide range of feature and television roles. We explore the complexities of her public image, from the heights of adoration to the depths of controversy, and examine the impact of her words and actions on the cultural landscape.

But beyond the glitz and glamour of Hollywood lies a woman of substance—a philanthropist, an advocate, and a devoted mother. We shine a spotlight on Fox's lesser-known endeavors, from her philanthropic work to her advocacy for mental health awareness, showcasing the depth and breadth of her contributions to society.

With "Unveiling Megan Fox," we cordially invite you to travel with us as we solve the puzzles and commemorate the victories of one of Hollywood's most alluring characters. Through candid interviews, insightful analysis, and rich storytelling, we offer a comprehensive portrait of Megan Fox—the actress, the icon, and the woman behind the myth.

So, buckle up and prepare to be immersed in the extraordinary world of Megan Fox—a world where beauty meets brains, where talent knows no bounds, and where the journey is just as captivating as the destination. Welcome to the fascinating, multifaceted universe of Megan Fox.

Chapter 1
Early Life and Childhood

Birth and Family Background

Megan Denise Fox came into this world on May 16, 1986, in the serene town of Oak Ridge, Tennessee. She was the beloved daughter of Gloria Darlene (née Cisson) and Franklin Thomas Fox, both of whom played pivotal roles in shaping her early years. Megan's family roots were modest yet filled with love and determination.

Childhood Experiences and Upbringing

In the quaint surroundings of Rockwood, Tennessee, Megan spent her early childhood years surrounded by the nurturing embrace of her family. However, the tranquility of her upbringing was disrupted when her parents, Gloria and Franklin, parted ways when Megan was a mere three years old. Despite the challenges that accompanied this separation, Megan found solace and stability in the unwavering love of her mother.

Following her parents' divorce, Megan's mother remarried, and Megan, along with her sister, embarked on a new chapter of their lives under the guidance of their mother and stepfather, Tony Tonachio. Yet, the specter of adversity loomed large in their household, as Megan candidly revealed the struggles she faced with her stepfather's abusive behavior. These early trials would later shape Megan's resilience and fortitude in the face of adversity.

Early Education and Interests

From a young age, Megan displayed a keen interest in the performing arts, a passion that would come to define her future endeavors. At the tender age of five, she embarked on her journey into the world of dance and drama, laying the foundation for her future career in Hollywood. Despite the challenges she faced at home, Megan's unwavering determination propelled her forward, fueling her pursuit of excellence in her chosen craft.

As she transitioned into her formative years, Megan's thirst for knowledge and self-expression led her to explore various avenues of creativity. From her involvement in school choruses to her participation in swimming competitions, Megan embraced every opportunity to hone her skills and showcase her talents.

However, Megan's educational journey was not without its obstacles. Battling with the pressures of adolescence, Megan found herself grappling with issues of self-esteem and mental health. Her struggles with an eating disorder and manic depression cast a shadow over her formative years, yet they also served as catalysts for her personal growth and resilience.

Despite the turmoil that surrounded her, Megan's indomitable spirit and unwavering resolve remained unshaken. With each passing hurdle, she emerged stronger and more determined than ever to carve out her path in the world.

As Megan embarked on her teenage years, she found herself at a crossroads, grappling with the complexities of identity and belonging. In the halls of her middle school, Megan faced the harsh realities of bullying and ostracization, yet she refused to be defined by the narrow confines of societal expectations. Embracing her true self, Megan forged connections with like-minded individuals who accepted her for who she was, paving the way for lifelong friendships and enduring bonds.

Megan's journey took a wild turn as she made her way through the turbulent waters of adolescence in the high school environment. Faced with the pressures of conformity and societal norms, Megan found herself at odds with her peers, grappling with feelings of alienation and isolation. But even in the face of chaos and uncertainty, Megan persisted in her quest for self-awareness and refused to let other people's limitations stop her.

As she approached the threshold of adulthood, Megan made a bold decision to chart her own course, breaking free from the confines of traditional education to pursue her dreams in the City of Angels. With unwavering determination and boundless ambition, she set her sights on the bright lights of Hollywood, ready to embark on a journey that would forever alter the course of her life.

The next chapter of Megan Fox's incredible journey delves into her quick ascent to fame and the many obstacles and victories she faced along the way. Join us as we unravel the mysteries of Megan's early life and childhood, exploring the formative experiences that shaped her into the iconic figure she is today.

Chapter 2
Pursuing Acting

Introduction to Acting and Early Roles

Megan Fox's journey into the world of acting traces back to her early years, filled with dreams and aspirations. Fox's need for artistic expression as a child led to an early inclination for the performing arts. This innate talent led her to pursue opportunities in acting, starting with local theater productions and school performances. Despite her young age, Fox's dedication and commitment to her craft were evident, as she immersed herself in dance and drama training from the tender age of five.

Transition to Hollywood

As Fox's passion for acting blossomed, she set her sights on Hollywood, the epicenter of the entertainment industry. With dreams of making it big on the silver screen, she embarked on a journey filled with hope and determination. At the age of 17, Fox took a bold step forward, leaving behind her hometown and venturing to Los Angeles, California, to pursue her acting ambitions. It was a pivotal moment in her life, marking the beginning of her quest for success in the fiercely competitive world of Hollywood.

Challenges and Setbacks

However, the path to stardom was far from smooth for Fox. Alongside the glitz and glamour of Hollywood, she encountered numerous challenges and setbacks that tested her resilience. From facing rejection in auditions to struggling to make ends meet, Fox experienced the harsh realities of the industry firsthand. Moreover, she grappled with personal demons, including battles with eating disorders and mental health issues, which added to the complexity of her journey.

Despite the obstacles in her path, Fox refused to be deterred, drawing strength from her unwavering passion for acting. With each setback, she emerged stronger and more determined than ever to achieve her dreams. Through perseverance and sheer grit, Fox gradually began to carve out a niche for herself in Hollywood, securing her early roles that showcased her talent and versatility as an actress.

As Fox's journey unfolds, it becomes clear that her path to success was paved with hard work, resilience, and unwavering determination. From humble beginnings to Hollywood fame, her story serves as a testament to the power of perseverance and the pursuit of one's passions amidst adversity.

Chapter 3

Breakthrough with "Transformers"

The turning point in Megan Fox's career came with her iconic role in the blockbuster film "Transformers." Michael Bay directed this action-packed extravaganza, which thrust Fox into the public eye and cemented her place among Hollywood's elite.

Casting as Mikaela Banes

Fox's journey to landing the role of Mikaela Banes, the feisty and fearless love interest of Shia LaBeouf's character in "Transformers," was nothing short of serendipitous. After catching the eye of director Michael Bay, Fox underwent a rigorous audition process, where her undeniable talent and on-screen presence shone through. Fox was chosen for the desired role by Bay because of her charisma and undeveloped talent.

As Mikaela Banes, Fox brought a perfect blend of beauty, wit, and toughness to the screen, captivating audiences worldwide. Her electrifying chemistry with co-star Shia LaBeouf added an extra layer of depth to the film, making their on-screen romance one of the most memorable aspects of "Transformers."

With "Transformers," Megan Fox not only showcased her acting prowess but also cemented her status as a bona fide action star. The film's massive success propelled Fox to superstardom, opening doors to a myriad of opportunities in the entertainment industry. It was a breakthrough moment that would forever change the trajectory of her career, marking the beginning of a new chapter filled with unprecedented fame and recognition.

Impact of "Transformers" on Fox's Caree

In the summer of 2007, Megan Fox burst onto the Hollywood scene like a firework, igniting screens around the world with her portrayal of Mikaela Banes in Michael Bay's explosive blockbuster, "Transformers." Cast alongside Shia LaBeouf, Fox embodied the role of the tough yet alluring gearhead with undeniable charisma and a magnetic screen presence. The film's massive success not only catapulted Fox into the spotlight but also launched her career to stratospheric heights.

With "Transformers," Fox became more than just an actress; she became a cultural phenomenon. Her portrayal of Mikaela Banes captured the hearts of audiences worldwide, earning her legions of fans and solidifying her status as a Hollywood A-lister. The film's box office triumphs and critical acclaim propelled Fox into the realm of superstardom, opening doors to a myriad of opportunities in the entertainment industry.

Controversies and Media Attention

However, along with the adoration and acclaim came the intense scrutiny of the media spotlight. Megan Fox's skyrocketing fame brought with it a barrage of controversies and tabloid headlines, thrusting her personal life into the public eye. From rumors of on-set tensions with director Michael Bay to candid interviews where Fox spoke out against Hollywood's objectification of women, she found herself at the center of a whirlwind of media attention.

One of the most notable controversies surrounding Fox during her time with the "Transformers" franchise was her departure from the series. Following the release of "Transformers: Revenge of the Fallen," Fox made headlines when she publicly criticized director Michael Bay, likening him to Hitler in an interview. This candid remark, coupled with reports of on-set tensions and disagreements, led to Fox's departure from the franchise.

Despite the controversies and media scrutiny, there's no denying the profound impact that "Transformers" had on Megan Fox's career. It served as a launching pad for her ascent to stardom and showcased her talents to the world. While the road to success may have been paved with challenges and controversies, Fox emerged from the experience stronger and more resilient than ever, ready to take on whatever the future held.

Chapter 4

Filmography

Megan Fox's filmography spans a wide range of genres, showcasing her versatility as an actress. From action-packed blockbusters to indie dramas, Fox has left her mark on the film industry with her memorable performances.

One of Fox's breakthrough roles came in 2007, when she starred as Mikaela Banes in Michael Bay's "Transformers." Her portrayal of the tough and resourceful mechanic opposite Shia LaBeouf's character garnered widespread attention and catapulted her to international fame. The success of "Transformers" not only solidified Fox as a bankable star but also established her as a sex symbol, with her sultry on-screen presence captivating audiences worldwide.

Following the success of "Transformers," Fox continued to showcase her action chops in films like "Transformers: Revenge of the Fallen" (2009) and "Jonah Hex" (2010). However, she also ventured into different genres, demonstrating her range as an actress. Jennifer's Body, a 2009 horror-comedy, starred Fox as the title character, a demon-possessed high school cheerleader. Her performance received praise for its blend of dark humor and vulnerability, showcasing Fox's ability to tackle complex roles.

In addition to her action and horror roles, Fox has also showcased her dramatic talents in films like "Friends with Kids" (2011) and "Passion Play" (2010). In "Friends with Kids," she played a single mother navigating the complexities of modern relationships, delivering a nuanced performance that resonated with audiences and critics alike. Similarly, in "Passion Play," Fox portrayed a carnival performer with wings, opposite Mickey Rourke, delving into themes of love, redemption, and self-discovery.

Analysis of Significant Roles and Performances

Throughout her career, Fox has displayed a willingness to challenge herself with diverse roles, showcasing her range as an actress. While she initially gained attention for her looks and action-oriented performances, she has since proven her acting prowess in a variety of genres.

One of Fox's most significant performances came in "Jennifer's Body," where she defied expectations by delivering a layered portrayal of a character struggling with her newfound demonic powers. Fox seamlessly balanced the film's comedic and horror elements, creating a memorable and multi-dimensional character that resonated with audiences.

Another standout role for Fox was in "Friends with Kids," where she demonstrated her ability to tackle more grounded and emotionally complex material. As a single mother navigating the challenges of co-parenting and romance, Fox brought depth and authenticity to her character, earning praise for her performance.

Evolution of Fox's Acting Style

Over the years, Megan Fox's acting style has evolved as she has taken on a diverse range of roles and honed her craft. While she initially gained attention for her roles in action-oriented blockbusters, she has since demonstrated her versatility by tackling more dramatic and comedic roles.

Early in her career, Fox's acting style was characterized by her confident and assertive on-screen presence, often embodying strong and independent female characters. However, as she has matured as an actress, Fox has shown a willingness to explore different facets of her talent, delving into more nuanced and emotionally resonant roles.

In recent years, Fox has gravitated towards projects that allow her to showcase her range as an actress, from indie dramas to offbeat comedies. Her willingness to take risks and push herself out of her comfort zone has endeared her to audiences and critics alike, cementing her status as one of Hollywood's most versatile and compelling actresses. As she continues to evolve and grow in her career, it's clear that Megan Fox's talent knows no bounds, and audiences can look forward to seeing her shine in a variety of roles for years to come.

Chapter 5
Television Career

Megan Fox's journey through the world of cinema is marked by a series of diverse roles that have showcased her versatility and talent. From her breakout role in "Transformers" to her more recent ventures into indie dramas, Fox has continually pushed the boundaries of her acting abilities, captivating audiences with her on-screen presence and charisma.

In 2007, Fox burst onto the scene with her portrayal of Mikaela Banes in Michael Bay's "Transformers." As the tough and resourceful mechanic, Fox brought a blend of strength and vulnerability to the character, earning praise for her ability to hold her own alongside seasoned action stars. The success of "Transformers" propelled Fox into the spotlight, making her one of Hollywood's most sought-after actresses virtually overnight.

Following the success of "Transformers," Fox continued to make her mark in the action genre with roles in films like "Transformers: Revenge of the Fallen" (2009) and "Jonah Hex" (2010). In these films, Fox showcased her ability to handle high-octane action sequences with ease, solidifying her reputation as a bona fide action star. However, she also demonstrated her range as an actress by exploring different genres and taking on more challenging roles.

One such role was in the 2009 horror-comedy "Jennifer's Body," where Fox played the titular character, a high school cheerleader possessed by a demon. In this film, Fox defied expectations by delivering a performance that was equal parts darkly humorous and emotionally resonant. Her portrayal of Jennifer garnered praise from critics and audiences alike, cementing her status as a versatile actress capable of tackling complex and multifaceted roles.

In addition to her work in action and horror films, Fox has also proven herself in the realm of drama with roles in films like "Friends with Kids" (2011) and "Passion Play" (2010). In "Friends with Kids," Fox portrayed a single mother navigating the challenges of modern relationships with honesty and authenticity. Her performance earned her accolades for its emotional depth and sincerity, showcasing her ability to excel in roles that require more subtle and nuanced acting.

Similarly, in "Passion Play," Fox took on the role of a carnival performer with wings, opposite Mickey Rourke. Despite the film's mixed reception, Fox's performance was widely praised for its ethereal quality and emotional resonance. In this role, Fox demonstrated her willingness to take risks and explore unconventional characters, further solidifying her reputation as an actress who is unafraid to challenge herself and push the boundaries of her craft.

Analysis of Significant Roles and Performances

Throughout her career, Megan Fox has delivered a series of memorable performances that have left a lasting impact on audiences and critics alike. One of her most significant roles came in "Jennifer's Body," where she portrayed the complex and conflicted character of Jennifer Check with depth and nuance. In this film, Fox showcased her ability to balance the film's comedic elements with its darker undertones, delivering a performance that was both chilling and captivating.

Another standout performance for Fox was in "Friends with Kids," where she portrayed the character of Mary Jane, a single mother grappling with the challenges of parenthood and romance. In this film, Fox demonstrated her range as an actress by infusing the character with vulnerability and authenticity, earning praise for her portrayal of a woman struggling to find her place in the world.

In addition to her dramatic roles, Fox has also excelled in action-oriented roles like Mikaela Banes in the "Transformers" franchise. In these films, Fox showcased her ability to handle complex action sequences with grace and agility, proving herself to be a capable action star in her own right.

Overall, Megan Fox's body of work reflects her versatility as an actress and her willingness to take risks in order to push herself as an artist. Whether she's portraying a tough-as-nails mechanic or a vulnerable single mother, Fox brings a level of authenticity and depth to her characters that resonates with audiences and critics alike. As she continues to evolve and grow in her career, it's clear that Megan Fox's talent knows no bounds, and audiences can look forward to seeing her shine in a variety of roles for years to come.

Chapter 6

Public Image and Persona

Megan Fox's public image has been shaped by a combination of her on-screen roles, personal life, and media portrayal. Since her rise to fame in the mid-2000s, Fox has often been perceived as a sex symbol, thanks in part to her stunning looks and sultry on-screen presence. However, behind the glamorous facade lies a complex and multifaceted individual who has faced both praise and criticism throughout her career.

Perception as a Sex Symbol

From the moment she burst onto the Hollywood scene, Megan Fox's physical appearance became a focal point of media attention. With her striking blue eyes, full lips, and hourglass figure, Fox quickly became synonymous with beauty and sensuality, earning her a reputation as one of Hollywood's most desirable women.

Much of Fox's early success can be attributed to her portrayal of strong and alluring female characters in films like "Transformers" and "Jennifer's Body." In these roles, Fox exuded confidence and sex appeal, captivating audiences with her smoldering on-screen presence. However, while her beauty undoubtedly helped propel her career, it also led to her being typecast and objectified by both the media and industry insiders.

Media Scrutiny and Challenges

Despite her undeniable talent as an actress, Megan Fox has often found herself the subject of intense media scrutiny and criticism. Throughout her career, she has been criticized for everything from her acting abilities to her personal life choices, with tabloids and gossip columns dissecting her every move.

One of the most infamous incidents of media scrutiny came in 2009, when Fox was fired from the "Transformers" franchise after publicly criticizing director Michael Bay. In an interview with Wonderland magazine, Fox compared Bay to Adolf Hitler, sparking outrage among fans and industry insiders alike. While Fox later clarified her comments and reconciled with Bay, the incident served as a stark reminder of the challenges she faced as a young woman in Hollywood.

In addition to facing criticism for her outspoken nature, Fox has also been the target of relentless objectification and sexism in the media. Throughout her career, she has been subjected to invasive paparazzi photos, tabloid rumors, and derogatory headlines, all of which have taken a toll on her mental and emotional well-being.

Personal Branding and Public Statements

In recent years, Megan Fox has taken control of her public image by rebranding herself as more than just a sex symbol. Through her social media presence and public statements, Fox has sought to reclaim her narrative and challenge societal expectations of beauty and femininity.

One way Fox has done this is by speaking out about her experiences in Hollywood and advocating for gender equality in the entertainment industry. In interviews and public appearances, Fox has been vocal about the challenges she has faced as a woman in a male-dominated industry, including instances of harassment and discrimination.

In addition to her advocacy work, Fox has also used her platform to promote body positivity and self-acceptance. Through candid Instagram posts and heartfelt interviews, Fox has opened up about her own struggles with body image and self-esteem, inspiring fans to embrace their flaws and celebrate their uniqueness.

Furthermore, Fox has also diversified her career by branching out into other ventures, including fashion design and philanthropy. In recent years, she has launched her own lingerie line and collaborated with various charitable organizations to support causes close to her heart, such as animal welfare and environmental conservation.

Megan Fox's public image and persona are a reflection of her journey as an actress and individual. While she initially gained fame as a sex symbol, Fox has since evolved into a multifaceted woman who is unafraid to challenge stereotypes and speak her truth. Despite facing intense media scrutiny and criticism, Fox has remained resilient in the face of adversity, using her platform to advocate for causes she believes in and inspire others to embrace their authentic selves. As she continues to navigate the ups and downs of fame, one thing is clear: Megan Fox is much more than just a pretty face—she's a force to be reckoned with.

Chapter 7

Personal Life

Megan Fox's personal life has been a subject of fascination for fans and tabloids alike. From her high-profile relationships to her struggles with mental health, Fox has faced numerous challenges in her journey to find happiness and fulfillment outside of the spotlight.

Relationships and Family

Throughout her career, Megan Fox has been romantically linked to several notable figures in Hollywood. In 2004, she started seeing actor Brian Austin Green, whom she met on the set of the sitcom "Hope & Faith." Despite their 12-year age difference, the couple's relationship blossomed, and they became engaged in 2006.

In 2010, Fox and Green tied the knot in a private ceremony in Hawaii. Over the years, the couple welcomed three sons together: Noah Shannon Green (born in 2012), Bodhi Ransom Green (born in 2014), and Journey River Green (born in 2016). Despite their growing family, Fox and Green's relationship faced its fair share of ups and downs, with the couple filing for divorce in 2015 before reconciling a year later.

In 2020, Fox and Green announced their separation once again, with Fox filing for divorce citing irreconcilable differences. Since then, Fox has been romantically linked to rapper Machine Gun Kelly, with whom she starred in the film "Midnight in the Switchgrass." The couple's relationship has garnered significant media attention, with Fox publicly declaring her love for Kelly and referring to him as her "twin flame."

Struggles with Mental Health and Self-esteem

Despite her success in Hollywood, Megan Fox has been open about her struggles with mental health and self-esteem. In interviews and public statements, Fox has spoken candidly about her experiences with anxiety, depression, and body dysmorphia, revealing the toll that fame and public scrutiny have taken on her mental and emotional well-being.

In a 2013 interview with Esquire magazine, Fox admitted to battling crippling anxiety and insecurity, confessing that she often felt like a "fraud" in Hollywood. She also opened up about her struggles with body image, revealing that she had undergone plastic surgery in an attempt to conform to society's standards of beauty.

In addition to her struggles with mental health, Fox has also faced criticism and backlash for her outspoken nature and unfiltered opinions. Throughout her career, she has been labeled everything from "difficult" to "unhinged" by the media, with tabloids often painting her as a troubled and controversial figure.

Despite the challenges she has faced, Fox has remained resilient in the face of adversity, using her platform to advocate for mental health awareness and self-acceptance. Through candid social media posts and heartfelt interviews, she has encouraged fans to embrace their flaws and celebrate their uniqueness, proving that even the most glamorous celebrities are not immune to the pressures of fame.

Philanthropy and Advocacy

In addition to her acting career, Megan Fox is also actively involved in philanthropy and advocacy work. Throughout the years, she has supported various charitable organizations and causes, using her platform to raise awareness and funds for issues close to her heart.

One cause that is particularly important to Fox is animal welfare. As a longtime animal lover and advocate, she has worked with organizations like the Humane Society and PETA to promote animal rights and combat animal cruelty. In 2017, Fox even launched her own charity initiative, the "Megan Fox Foundation," which aims to provide resources and support to animal shelters and rescue organizations.

In addition to her work with animals, Fox is also passionate about environmental conservation and sustainability. She has spoken out about the importance of protecting the planet for future generations, advocating for measures to combat climate change and promote renewable energy sources.

Furthermore, Fox is also an advocate for LGBTQ+ rights and equality. In interviews and public statements, she has expressed her support for the LGBTQ+ community, calling for greater acceptance and inclusion in society. She has also used her platform to speak out against discrimination and prejudice, emphasizing the importance of love and acceptance for all individuals, regardless of sexual orientation or gender identity.

Chapter 8
Beyond Acting

Megan Fox's talents extend far beyond the silver screen, with her diverse interests and ventures making a significant impact both within and beyond the entertainment industry. From fashion design to activism, Fox has proven herself to be a multifaceted individual with a passion for creativity and social change.

Other Ventures and Interests

In addition to her acting career, Megan Fox has explored various other ventures and interests, showcasing her entrepreneurial spirit and creative vision. One of her notable ventures is her foray into fashion design, where she has collaborated with several clothing brands to create her own collections.

In 2009, Fox partnered with the fashion brand Frederick's of Hollywood to launch her own lingerie line, "Megan Fox for Frederick's of Hollywood." The collection featured a range of sultry lingerie pieces inspired by Fox's signature style, combining elegance with a hint of edginess. The line was well-received by fans and critics alike, showcasing Fox's eye for design and her ability to create fashion-forward pieces that empower women to embrace their femininity.

Outside of fashion, Fox has also explored her passion for writing, penning articles and essays on topics ranging from motherhood to mental health. In 2018, she published an autobiographical essay titled "I'm Not Your Bunny Boiler, Baby," where she reflected on her experiences in Hollywood and challenged stereotypes about women in the industry. The essay received praise for its candidness and insight, further establishing Fox as a voice for empowerment and self-expression.

Impact Beyond the Entertainment Industry

Beyond her work in film and fashion, Megan Fox has also made a significant impact through her activism and philanthropic efforts. Throughout the years, she has supported various charitable organizations and causes, using her platform to raise awareness and funds for issues close to her heart.

One cause that is particularly important to Fox is environmental conservation. As a passionate advocate for sustainability, she has spoken out about the importance of protecting the planet for future generations, advocating for measures to combat climate change and promote renewable energy sources. In 2019, Fox teamed up with the environmental organization Sierra Club to launch the "Megan

Fox Green Initiative," which aims to raise awareness about environmental issues and promote eco-friendly practices.

In addition to her environmental activism, Fox is also an outspoken advocate for animal rights. As a longtime animal lover and supporter of organizations like the Humane Society and PETA, she has used her platform to raise awareness about animal cruelty and promote adoption from animal shelters. In 2020, Fox even adopted a vegan lifestyle, citing ethical and environmental concerns as motivating factors.

Fox furthermore supports equality and rights for LGBTQ+ people. Her support for the LGBTQ+ community and her call for increased acceptance and inclusion in society have been made clear in interviews and public remarks. She has also used her platform to speak out against discrimination and prejudice, emphasizing the importance of love and acceptance for all individuals, regardless of sexual orientation or gender identity.

Chapter 9

Legacy and Influence

Megan Fox's impact on Hollywood and popular culture is undeniable, with her career spanning over two decades and leaving a lasting imprint on the entertainment industry. From her breakthrough roles in blockbuster films to her advocacy for social change, Fox has become a cultural icon whose influence extends far beyond the confines of the silver screen.

Megan Fox burst onto the Hollywood scene in the mid-2000s, captivating audiences with her striking looks and magnetic on-screen presence. Her breakout role as Mikaela Banes in Michael Bay's "Transformers" catapulted her to international fame, establishing her as one of Hollywood's most sought-after actresses virtually overnight. With her sultry beauty and undeniable talent, Fox quickly became synonymous with the image of the modern-day femme fatale, redefining traditional notions of femininity and sexuality in mainstream cinema.

Throughout her career, Fox has challenged stereotypes and broken barriers, paving the way for a new generation of actresses to follow in her footsteps. Her portrayal of strong and independent female characters has inspired countless fans around the world, empowering women to embrace their strength and their uniqueness. Whether she's fighting giant robots in "Transformers" or battling demons in "Jennifer's

Body," Fox has consistently pushed the boundaries of what it means to be a leading lady in Hollywood, proving that women can be both fierce and feminine.

In addition to her impact on the silver screen, Megan Fox has also left a mark on popular culture through her fashion choices, social media presence, and outspoken advocacy. With millions of followers on platforms like Instagram and Twitter, Fox has leveraged her platform to raise awareness about important issues like mental health, environmental conservation, and LGBTQ+ rights. Her candidness and authenticity have endeared her to fans around the world, making her a relatable and inspirational figure for a new generation of women.

Reflections on Her Career and Contributions

As Megan Fox reflects on her career and contributions to Hollywood, she remains grateful for the opportunities she has been afforded and the experiences that have shaped her journey. From her humble beginnings as a young actress struggling to make ends meet to her meteoric rise to fame as one of Hollywood's most recognizable faces, Fox acknowledges the highs and lows of her career with humility and grace.

Throughout the years, Fox has faced her fair share of challenges and setbacks, from being typecast as a sex symbol to enduring intense media scrutiny and criticism. However, she has also experienced moments of triumph and personal growth, finding strength in adversity and using her platform to advocate for causes she believes in. As she looks back on her career, Fox is proud of the impact she has had on popular culture and the positive change she has inspired in the world.

Moving forward, Megan Fox remains committed to pushing boundaries and challenging norms, both in her career and in her personal life. With several exciting projects on the horizon, including new film roles and fashion collaborations, Fox is eager to continue exploring her creativity and pursuing her passions. As she embarks on the next chapter of her journey, one thing is certain: Megan Fox's legacy will endure for generations to come, inspiring audiences to embrace their uniqueness and strive for greatness in all that they do.

Conclusion

To conclude, Megan Fox's story is one of resilience, passion, and empowerment. From her humble beginnings to her rise to international fame, Fox has navigated the highs and lows of Hollywood with grace and determination. Through her diverse roles, bold fashion choices, and unwavering advocacy, she has challenged stereotypes, broken barriers, and inspired millions around the world.

As we reflect on Fox's journey, we are reminded of the power of authenticity and the importance of staying true to oneself in the face of adversity. Her willingness to speak out about important issues like mental health, environmental conservation, and LGBTQ+ rights has made her not only a cultural icon but also a force for positive change.

Using Megan Fox as an example, let us carry forward Megan Fox's legacy of empowerment and inspiration. Let us continue to challenge norms, embrace our uniqueness, and strive for greatness in all that we do. As Megan Fox herself once said, "I don't want to have to be like a Scarlett Johansson — who I have nothing against, but I don't want to have to go, 'You know, I can do that too.' I don't want to have to prove that I can act or that I can be this. I just want to be given the chance to express myself and be who I am."

In the end, Megan Fox's journey reminds us that the greatest success comes from staying true to ourselves and using our voices to create positive change in the world.

Printed in Great Britain
by Amazon